Roger Guttridge was born in 1950 and was brought up in the heart of the Blackmore Vale, where his maternal ancestors have lived for centuries. His grandfather, Jim Ridout of Fiddleford, appears in two of the pictures dating from the First and Second World Wars. Roger Guttridge was educated at Sturminster Newton Primary School and Blandford Grammar School, where a school project on his smuggling ancestors from Okeford Fitzpaine introduced him to historical research and led, fifteen years later, to his first book, *Dorset Smugglers*. He worked as a journalist for *The Western Gazette* for five years and the *Bournemouth Evening Echo* for fifteen and is now a freelance writer based at Wimborne. His other books include *Dorset Murders*, *Ten Dorset Mysteries*, and *Six Men on the Stour* (by Ernest J. Brett). He also writes the popular Heritage columns in the *Bournemouth* and *Southern Evening Echoes*.

1. Haymaking near Marnhull in about 1900.

5 Knotts Close,
Child Okeford,
Blandford Forum,
Dorset. DT11 8ES
Phone 0258 860393

BLACKMORE VALE CAMERA

ROGER GUTTRIDGE

THE DOVECOTE PRESS

2. One of the earliest known pictures of Sturminster Newton showing the White Hart in the 1860s. The building bears the date 1708, proving that it survived the fire which destroyed most of the town centre in 1729. The late Ray Rogers noted that in the early 1900s a waiter called Mullins used to stand outside the White Hart at noon on market days and announce in a loud voice: "Dinners ready – one shillin'!"

First published in 1991 by the Dovecote Press Ltd
Stanbridge, Wimborne, Dorset BH21 4JD

Designed by the Dovecote Press Ltd
Photoset by The Typesetting Bureau Ltd, Wimborne, Dorset
Origination by Chroma Graphics (Overseas) Pte Ltd, Singapore
Printed by Kim Hup Lee Printing Co Pte Ltd, Singapore

British Library Cataloguing-in-Publication Data
A catalogue record for this book is
available from the British Library

ISBN 0 946159 90 4

Contents

Introduction

In the introduction to my first book, *Dorset Smugglers,* I wrote that researching for it had been a voyage of discovery. Eight years and several books later I can state with equal sincerity that *Blackmore Vale Camera* has provided a voyage of rediscovery, for it has put me in touch with my roots. The search for pictures and information about them has taken me to villages which were once familiar territory but which I have seen little of in the last twenty years. It has also renewed acquaintanceships and revived many memories from my early years. The photograph of Harding's fire at Sturminster in particular brought back vivid memories. I was a boy of six when the newsagent's shop in Bridge Street was burnt down and I remember picking my way through the debris on my way to school the following morning. It made a deep impression on me then and the memory has stayed with me for thirty-five years, rekindled every time I have attended a fire as a reporter and smelt once again the unmistakable stench of burnt and smouldering property.

Photographs of Sturminster Market also brought memories flooding back, for it played a significant part in my childhood; so too did pictures of past carnivals and of the railway on which I travelled to school at Blandford until Dr Beeching had his way. Then there were the years that I sang with the Sturminster church choir, the gigs with a pop group at Hazelbury Bryan, the village dances at Stalbridge, the school holiday jobs at King's Stag, Okeford Fitzpaine and Shillingstone. Almost every village in the Blackmore Vale offers its own special memories, but many of the pictures which hold personal memories for me have not made it as far as the printer, for the final selection was made from a shortlist of hundreds. Those selected cover 130 years of local history and have been chosen to represent a broad spectrum of life in the Blackmore Vale.

When the earliest picture in this book was taken, Queen Victoria was barely half-way through her long reign, Lord Palmerston was Prime Minister and *Our Mutual Friend* was the latest offering from the nineteenth century's most popular novelist Charles Dickens. Locally the steam train had recently made its debut on the newly-completed Somerset and Dorset Railway, Bagber's most famous son William Barnes had taken up his new duties as Rector of Winterborne

Came and in London a young architect from Dorset called Thomas Hardy was taking his first tentative steps along the road to a literary career.

In the Blackmore Vale, as in most of Dorset, rural life was proceeding much as it had done for centuries. Some parts of England had endured immense social and environmental change in the first half of the nineteenth century as the industrial revolution swept all before it. But industry had given a fairly wide berth to an area which had already escaped canalmania (albeit narrowly, for eight miles of the Somerset and Dorset Canal were built before it was abandoned for want of funds). Agriculture was still the dominant industry in North Dorset, providing — directly or indirectly — employment for a large percentage of the working population. But there were major changes in store, even for agriculture, and the photographs in this book cover the transition from manual labour, through the steam age, to the period of rapid mechanisation which followed the First World War.

The Great War itself was a momentous event which left no family untouched, in North Dorset or anywhere else. There is no more poignant picture in *Blackmore Vale Camera* than that of the people of Marnhull gathered for the departure of the young men of the village in August 1914. The soldiers, young and inexperienced, left with hope and confidence in their hearts, swept along on the tidal wave of national euphoria which then prevailed. The war would be over by Christmas, they were told; but it wasn't, and the fond farewell outside Marnhull's Crown Inn was destined for many to be a last goodbye.

The Great War precipitated many changes and agriculture was not the only aspect of life to be subjected to rapid mechanisation. On the roads the horse gave way to the superior horse power of the internal combustion engine and this in turn generated the need for roads to be given a metalled surface. "The arrival of the road gang caused great excitement in the village," David Wilkins of Marnhull recalls. Other changes accompanied the improvements in roads and transport — such as telephone kiosks, wireless sets, mains electricity. The Dorset of Barnes and Young and Hardy was suddenly left far behind.

The photographs which follow reflect many of these

changes, providing a rich visual record of the most eventful period in the history of the Blackmore Vale. In many cases the photographers who took them are unidentified and probably destined to remain so. An exception to this is the firm of Clarke and Son, photographers, of Sturminster Newton and Stalbridge, who were quite prolific in their production of picture postcards of the area in the early years of this century. Unfortunately their choice of photographic chemicals left a lot to be desired, with the result that almost all their pictures have faded over the years. Fortunately most have not faded sufficiently to put them beyond the reach of modern technology.

ROGER GUTTRIDGE

Acknowledgements

One of the great joys of collecting material for this book has been the extraordinary willingness of people to provide photographs and information about them. Of the many people I have approached, all but one have gone out of their way to be helpful to the extent, in most cases, of allowing me to borrow their pictures for several months. One very sweet old gentleman even took several framed pictures off the wall of his study, trusting me to return them when they were no longer required!

My starting point was the remarkable photographic collection of the late Raymond Rogers and I am particularly grateful to Gwyneth Rogers, without whose co-operation this book would have been difficult if not impossible to complete. I am equally grateful to Barry Cuff, whose Dorset collection is just as remarkable, to David Wilkins and Chris Eyres, whose collections on Marnhull and Hazelbury Bryan respectively have been invaluable, and to all the undermentioned who have provided photographs and information.

Mrs Gwyneth Rogers, photograph numbers: 2, 3, 4, 5, 7, 8, 10, 15, 17, 19, 20, 21, 22, 25, 37, 48, 69, 70, 71, 72, 73, 87, 88, 98, 105, 109, 110, 112, 116, 118, 120, 134, 136, 138, 152; Mr Barry Cuff 11, 12, 13, 14, 16, 18, 29, 53, 57, 59, 64, 74, 78, 81, 82, 84, 85, 96, 103, 117, 119, 126, 129, 130, 131, 132, 139, 145, 146, 148, 150, 151; Mr David Wilkins 1, 26, 27, 28, 42, 43, 44, 52, 54, 55, 56, 63, 65, 66, 67, 68, 89, 90, 91, 92, 97, 106, 114, 115, 121, 123, 124, 128, 133, 143; Mr Chris Eyres 45, 47; Mr Chris Eyres and Mr David Hobson 36, 87, 99, 101, 122, 142; Mr Chris Eyres and Mr Philip Ellwood 50; Mrs Grace Frizell 34, 76, 94, 95, 108, back cover; Mrs Linda Hayward 32, 33, 102, 147; Mr and Mrs Arthur Field 35, 38, 39, 49, 77, 136, 137, front cover; Mr Percy Dike 93, 104, 113, 141; Mr William Dike 86; Mr and Mrs Lionel Wallis 40, 60; Miss Heather Fox 46, 51, 107, 135; Mr Ivor Ridout 31, 58, 80, 140, 144; Mr and Mrs Dennis and Freda White 23; Mrs J. S. Hughes 75; Mrs Connie Guttridge 9, 79; Mrs Rosa Oliver 62; Mrs Kay Old 30, 125, 149; Mr and Mrs Charles and Barbara Smith 24; Mr Paul Geal 83; Mr and Mrs Ron Barter 100; Mrs I. K. Lodge 127; Messrs H & J Eckardt 111; Mr David Lloyd 41, 61.

I am also grateful to the following for information needed for captions: Mr and Mrs Cyril and Enid Knott, Mr Ray Matthews; Mr Tom Hillier, Mrs Linda Wild, Mr and Mrs John Barnes, Mr Tom Fox, Mrs Irene Jones, Mr Dick Hunt, Mr and Mrs Brian Oliver, Misses Mary and Hilda Clarke.

3. Workmen outside Sturminster Newton Methodist Church in the summer of 1914.

The Market Town

4. Carts and traps in the Market Place on a market day in about 1906. In past centuries the Market Place was just that and at one time market day was Thursday. In 1774 sheep and calves were sold outside the Swan, horses outside what is now Lloyds' Bank and pigs in Church Street. At times in the past two cows were kept close by the market and led around to comply with a condition that cattle must be available for sale or the right to hold a market would be forfeited.

5, 6. Two views of the market, in about 1910 (*top*) and in 1990 (*bottom*). The market has long been the lifeblood of Sturminster Newton, hence the recent concerted campaign to prevent its closure and redevelopment. The town's market rights date back at least to 1332, when Edward III signed a charter permitting two two-day and two three-day street fairs each year. The charter also mentions a display of horses yoked for ploughing on the first day and entertainment on the second day of the two-day fair and agrees to requests for a "livestock market, especially a pig market". Henry VII signed another charter in 1496 referring to Sturminster's "thriving livestock market with a street fair and market combined". Today's livestock market is said to include the biggest calf market in Britain.

7. The heartbreaking scene at Sturminster market in 1935 as 2,000 carcasses are burnt following an outbreak of foot and mouth disease. The Ministry of Agriculture banned the movement of all livestock at the market following the discovery of two infected calves. The mass slaughter involved 896 cattle, 778 pigs and 326 sheep, and 60 tons of coal were bought to fuel the burning in trenches dug by local labour. The modern calf sheds were later built on the site.

8. The Rivers Arms Hotel at the turn of the century. It stands opposite the market in Station Road and at one time the market business spilled over into the pub yard and forecourt, where pets, plants and bric-a-brac could be bought.

9. "In the centre of the town," wrote Sir Frederick Treves in 1906 with typically caustic humour, "is the semblance of a square, to which all roads lead. Here an officious gas standard carrying aloft the latest pattern of lamp, the stump of an ancient stone cross, and the town pump. The latter is of wood, is small, black and vixenish. On it is a notice spitefully warning the passer-by that he will be prosecuted if he does it hurt, and adding further that no children must use the exclusive structure. There is a sourness in this, for all children delight to play with pumps."

10. The town pump was replaced within a few years of Treves's visit by a drinking fountain and horse trough which today serves as a flower box. It was erected in memory of Dr John Comyns Leach JP, who practised in Sturminster for more than 40 years and died aged 65 in 1907, and his son, E. Comyns Leach, a surgeon who died in Sierra Leone in 1902 aged 33. The area around it remains a handy pitch for market traders like this man selling garden and livestock equipment in 1948.

11. Sturminster Market Place in about 1905 showing the gas lamp erected to mark the coronation of Edward VII in 1902. By 1909 a single lamp had replaced the double one; by 1930 there was a double lamp again.

12. Carts and wagons, cycles, motor cycles and a pram clutter the Market Place at Sturminster Newton during the First World War. The Swan Hotel has changed little in 75 years.

13. *(Left)* Looking up White Lane (now Bath Road) from Sturminster Square in 1904. The house on the site of today's public library was then a coffee shop.

14. *(Below)* Rixton Hill, Sturminster Newton, in about 1905.

15. *(Right)* Residents of Penny Street, Sturminster Newton, pose for the photographer in 1895. William Barnes the poet would have passed this way on his way to school or the home of his patron Mr Dashwood. The people on the footpath are (from left) H. Marsh, Mr Roberts, Mrs Marsh (kneeling), Ted Marsh and Sid Courage (babies), Mrs Courage (in pinafore), Mrs Roberts, Miss G. and Miss E. Manlin.

16. *(Below)* Looking up Bridge Street, Sturminster, about 1920 with hatter and outfitter Harry Lemon's shop on the left. The parked wagon bears the date 1903 and the name of Rossiter, builder.

17. One of Sturminster Newton's most prized assets is the six-arch Town Bridge over the Stour with its famous plaque threatening transportation to anyone damaging it. The bridge was built in the 15th or early 16th century and widened from 12 to 18 feet in 1820. The earlier of its two date stones (1820 and 1827) has been placed upside down on the central upstream cutwater so that it can be read by anyone leaning over the parapet. The two white cottages in the background were demolished in the 1970s.

18. Sturminster bridge viewed from the footpath to Newton in 1907. At that time the path ran from the bridge to the top of Newton Hill avoiding the main road but it was later closed due to the danger from landslips. Approach roads to the bridge were lined by railings and white posts to ensure safe passage when the river flooded.

19. Tom Knott drawing water from the River Stour near Sturminster bridge in about 1930. The pump was erected to the west of the bridge in 1870 following a vote at the parish meeting. "This will place a supply of water within reach of many families who are now almost destitute of that necessity of life," the Western Gazette reported.

20. The once-in-a-century scene at Sturminster bridge in January 1963 when a hindquarter of beef was roasted on the Stour during the "big freeze". The ice was nine inches thick and hundreds (including myself) turned out for the rare experience of walking on the river. "While the roasting was proceeding there was skating and ice hockey and later, as darkness fell, dancing on the river under floodlights to amplified music," reported the Western Gazette. A similar ox-roasting was held between Colber Bridge and the railway bridge in 1895.

21. A pony and trap waits outside the Bull Inn at Sturminster Newton in about 1905. The landlord was George Dowling. Behind the Bull was a slaughterhouse and animal pound. In the 1880s a local man, Steven Adams, set up a stall outside the Bull each September offering sweets and cakes to people on their way to the famous Shroton Fair. His enterprise was known derisively as Bridge Fair!

22. A view of Newton, Sturminster's "other half", in about 1905. The Red Lion is the lighter coloured building right of centre. The tiled building behind the vegetation and wooden fence was soon to become the first Harvey's Garage, forerunner of the same family's present motor repair business in Bath Road.

Churches and Schools

23. Workmen carrying out repairs and restoration work at St Peter's Church, Hinton St Mary, in 1893. The work included major repairs to the roof, east gable and chancel. The workmen include stonemason Ted White (right), who worked for the Pitt-Rivers Estate and lived in an estate cottage behind the White Horse pub. A more extensive restoration was carried out in 1908 by the Blandford builders C. N. Green at a cost of £559 10s 6d.

24. The Church of St Eustace, Ibberton, following its decline and final collapse in 1889. It was restored between 1902 and 1909 at a cost of £1,500. For most of the intervening period services were held in a specially-built corrugated iron building which today serves as the village hall.

25. The bells of Shillingstone church after their removal for retuning and rehanging by Taylor's of Loughborough in 1929. The beam on the right was eaten away by woodworm and replaced. A new cast-iron frame was also added. Ringer Charlie Stride (far left) was killed during the Second World War.

26. New Street, Marnhull, showing the original Wesleyan Chapel opened in 1829. It was built on the site of woolstapler William Lewis's woolcombing shed in which the first generation of Marnhull Methodists held their services. Lewis became the prime mover of early Methodism in the village after hearing a visiting preacher at the Burton Street crossroads. The first chapel had a gallery where a variety of musical instruments were played during services, including the viol, euphonium, flute, cornet, bassoon and clarinet.

27. The "new" Wesleyan Chapel opened on another site in New Street, Marnhull, in 1904. "A large marquee was erected in the field called Butts and tea was provided for Methodists who came from far and near," wrote Margaret Wilkins, who remembered the opening. "It was closed for services when Methodist union took place."

28. *(Above)* Boys from Marnhull School show off their latest crop at the village allotments in about 1930. Gardening had a significant slot in the school timetable between the wars and each boy had his own vegetable plot measuring about 10 feet by 20 feet. In wet weather the boys studied the theory of gardening; in the spring, summer and autumn they put the theory in practice. The girls, meanwhile, learnt cookery and needlecraft.

29. *(Left)* The National School at Lydlinch, founded in 1870. The school bell has now disappeared, the chimney is cemented over and the roof has acquired dormer windows but the building survives as a private house.

30. Ibberton School apparently photographed during the re-thatching of the roof before the First World War. The school closed about 1941, when the pupils were transferred to Woolland. Today they go to Hazelbury Bryan. The school building next to the Crown Inn has since been converted to a private house.

31. *(Above)* Childe Okeford School in the High Street in about 1905. The buildings were replaced by houses in the 1970s, when a new school opened in Station Road.

32. *(Left)* Folke School in 1915. The children are sporting medals probably given for regular attendance.

33. Children at Bishop's Caundle School celebrate Empire Day in 1931. "It was a longstanding tradition at the school to dress up as people from different parts of the British Empire," says Mrs Linda Hayward (nee Foot), the girl with the 'X' over her head.

34. *(Below)* Children at Pulham School in about 1933. The teachers are Ida Perrett (left) and Mrs Lavinia Clarke. The children clearly span an age range of several years and the younger ones in the front two rows have building blocks on their desks. The school building is now a dwelling.

35. *(Left)* The infants class at Sturminster Newton Council School around the time of its opening in Bridge Street in 1925. The school opened with 127 pupils and seven teachers, including two students. "We had more classrooms, better apparatus, more teachers and there followed for me a very happy time, though we all had to work very very hard," founding headmistress Miss Maggie Rose, formerly head of Sturminster Church of England Girls' and Infants' School, recalled years later. Many of the children pictured went on to become well-known characters locally. They are (back row) Jim Fish, Leslie Stockley, Reg Short, George Northover, Bob Newman, Eddie Maidment, Freddie Pope; (front) Cliffy Rowland, Gladys Pope, Edna Drake, Sylvie Bennett, Marge Joyce, Stan Spicer, Meine Drake, Vera Stockley. The teacher is Miss E. Rolls (or Wells), one of the students.

On the Farm

36. A labourer takes a break from haymaking to pose for the camera. The jar probably contains cider. The leaning post is a genuine Dorset wagon.

37. Hauling timber at Sturminster Newton at the turn of the century.

38. Walter Field working the area's first portable steam engine in the Recreation Field at Okeford Fitzpaine in about 1884. The engine – a Bryant and May Portable – is drawing its water from a tub and driving a threshing machine.

39. *(Following page)* A steam engine hauls threshing tackle past Hanford Cottages near Childe Okeford in about 1885. The engine – possibly a Wallis and Stevens – belonged to Sir Randolf Baker's Ranston Estate at Shroton and would have been moving the equipment from one farm to another. The cottages have changed little in 100 years.

40. *(Above)* One man went to mow – in this case young Bill Wallis, seen scything corn at Hibbet Bottom, Okeford Fitzpaine, in 1930.

41. *(Above)* Walter Lloyd with 'College Dawn' at East Stour in about 1910. Walter spent most of his working life as a groom at the Compton Stud at nearby Sandley. The church and house in the picture survive but the postbox has gone.

42. *(Below)* Cutting hay in the Blackmore Vale in about 1900.

43, 44. *(Opposite page)* Two photographs of haymakers at Ashley Farm, Marnhull, 1888.

45. *(Opposite page)* The Hunt family show off their new elevator and Lister "L" engine while building a hayrick at Spire Hill Farm, near Stalbridge, in 1914. Lister engines were made at Dursley, Gloucestershire.

46. *(Above)* Farmworkers in a hayfield at Okeford Fitzpaine enjoy the standard Blackmore Vale labourer's lunch of bread and cheese washed down with home-fermented cider. The date is about 1930; the line-up (from left) is George Clark, Tom Hillier, Harry Kerley, –?, Jim Ridout.

47. *(Below)* Cutting and binding corn in about 1917, possibly at Spire Hill Farm, near Stalbridge. The workers are old men and children, a common sight when most of the young men were serving their country in the Great War. The tractor towing the binder is a Fordson Model F, probably one of the first of 7,000 imported in 1917 under the Lease-lend scheme by which the United States assisted Britain towards the end of the war. Horses were scarce as well as men and the conversion to mechanisation helped to boost food production.

48. Cider-making at Dominey's Farm, Fiddleford, in about 1927, supervised by farmer Harry Rose with son Dick turning the handle and Harry Goddard shovelling the apples. Many North Dorset farming folk kept a barrel of the rough stuff in a handy barn or outhouse.

49. King Feisal, the boy King of Iraq, feeding oats into a threshing machine at Bagber in about 1947. Behind him is his tutor, Captain Julian Pitt-Rivers, of the Manor House, Hinton St Mary, where the young king was staying. In 1958, at the age of 23, King Feisal was murdered in Baghdad during a bloody coup which also claimed the lives of his powerful uncle, Crown Prince Abdulillah, and their Prime Minister, who was kicked to death by the mob.

The Vale at Work

50. Saddler and harness maker Frank Ellwood outside his shop at Partway, Hazelbury Bryan, which he bought from J Gillingham in about 1911. The lower sign advertises ropes, leggings, gloves, belts, braces, and trunks and leather cases "made to order and repaired", as well as light and heavy harness, saddles, clothing and stable requisites. Mr Ellwood left Hazelbury following his marriage in 1924 and continued in business from his wife's village shop at Thornford. By then the rise of motor transport was already forcing the saddlery trade into a sharp decline.

51. The Smithy at Okeford Fitzpaine in about 1920. It stood at High Bench where the Forge Garage is today. The blacksmith Joe Fox (left) was assisted by his brother Reuben.

52. A horse is shod at Alf Bastable's forge in New Street, Marnhull, in the 1920s. Bastable was also the landlord of the Queen's Head. The forge was almost opposite Andrews Brothers' cycle and electrical shop. It was demolished in the post-war years and replaced by sheltered housing for the elderly.

53. Bishop's Caundle in 1906 showing the workforce of James Eyres and Sons the blacksmiths

54. Basketmaker Edwin Drew in his workshop behind the Retreat Inn at Marnhull in 1955. He used to cut his own rushes from the River Stour and plait them to make mats, baskets and similar goods. Rushing was once a flourishing industry in Marnhull, originally led by the Cressy family, who employed cottagers to plait the rushes. Edwin Drew continued working into his 80s and was succeeded by Jack Crew.

55. Marnhull Brewery and Malthouse at Hillside, Marnhull, where ale and beer were made first by the Burt family, later the Jennings, then Jennings and Baker and finally Styring, White and Company. The firm absorbed the nearby Poplar Elm Brewery before itself being taken over by Hall and Woodhouse in about 1925, when the brewing was transferred to Blandford. A story is told of how children from Seniors Farm were often sent to Marnull Brewery to buy barm for their mother, who used it with other ingredients to make a non-alcoholic drink called "botanic beer". From Sturminster Newton came Fred and Edwin Cowley to buy barm for Aunt Ann Cowley's breadmaking. The building on the left of the picture was converted to flats.

56. A horse waits patiently for its wagon to be loaded at Sturminster Mill in the 1930s. The mill closed in 1970 but its machinery, dating from the beginning of the century, is now in action again as a working tourist attraction. The mill-hand's cottage (left), however, fell down many years ago.

57. Fiddleford Mill pictured from an unusual angle with its waterwheel in full flow. This was the mill of 31-stone Job Rose, immortalised as Worthy Bloom the Miller in the poetry of William Barnes.

58. Miller Frank Rickman at Bere Marsh Mill, Shillingstone, in about 1885. Rickman also owned mills at Blandford and Durweston. Shillingstone Mill closed in 1923 and today only traces of it remain.

59, 60. Butter and cheesemaking were traditionally a cottage industry but a century or so ago factories sprang up in several North Dorset towns and villages. One of the biggest was at Okeford Fitzpaine, where Edward "Neddy" Phillips founded his Hill View Dairies, seen here in 1907. Lionel Wallis recalls that his grandfather David Pope used to accompany Phillips as he travelled around the farms buying milk and cheese. The lower photograph shows cheesemakers at work in the factory in 1958. They are (from left) Lionel Wallis, Bobby Hargrave, Bill Bealing, Stan Bee and Eddie Cluett. The factory closed in 1973 and is now a chicken processing plant.

61. A carpenter's workshop at Stour Row in 1903. The workers are thought to be (from left) James Kiddle, Bill Hull, Bert Pike, Jimmy Pike and Jimmy Pike senior.

62. The receiving platform at Sturminster Newton Creamery in about 1916. The creamery was opened by a consortium of local farmers in 1913, when much of the milk was turned into cheese and sent by train to London. The man in the cart, Mr King, at one time delivered Sturminster's milk on foot, carrying yoked churns on a twice-daily three-hour round. The cheesemaker in the white coat is my grandfather, Jim Ridout, who later returned to the factory at Okeford Fitzpaine. Sturminster factory was taken over by the Milk Marketing Board in 1937 when 145 farmers were supplying milk. It survives today as a Dairy Crest factory whose products include award-winning Cheddar cheese.

63. Men from E. G. Wilkins' Marnhull-based building firm working in the mud at Fifehead Magdalen in the 1920s. "They used to say that your clothes got wet in November and didn't dry out until May," says David Wilkins. The original Wilkins company was founded by carpenter George Wilkins in the 1830s. In the 1870s, during an agricultural depression, his son Walter walked to Yorkshire and learned the trade of stonemason. Then he returned to practise his skill in his native village, where many buildings appeared in a distinctive Yorkshire style. An accident eventually forced Walter out of business but his son Edwin launched another company, E. G. Wilkins.

64. A travelling knife-grinder plies his trade at King's Stag in 1904. The Green Man has changed little in 87 years though it has lost the central chimney.

Shops and Shopkeepers

65, 66. Hayter's Stores and Bakery in Burton Street, Marnhull, were gutted and five horses burnt to death in a fire which broke out during the night of March 1-2, 1909. In the absence of telephones a messenger, George Turner, had to cycle to Gillingham to alert the fire brigade, who arrived in time to save the adjoining Queen's Head Inn. The lower photograph shows the premises after rebuilding by W. Wilkins. Today a chemist occupies the building.

67, 68. Inside Hayter's grocery and drapery shops before the 1909 fire. Some of the names prominently displayed in the general store are still familiar today – Hovis, Nestle's, Camp coffee and Wills' Gold Flake. The drapery section appears to be selling carpets as well as ladies' apparel.

69. *(Above)* In 1972 fire put an end to another long-established family business, the ironmongers T. W. Barnett and Sons at Sturminster Newton Market Cross. The business was founded a century or so earlier and is here seen in 1913. Two doors away the Red Rose Restaurant of today (background, right) was occupied by Young Brothers, saddlers.

70. *(Below)* The top of Bridge Street, Sturminster Newton, in about 1920. The shop on the right – called Prospect House – was occupied by H. C. Bracher, a basket and chair maker. He used to pull his raw materials from the withy bed near the river bridge and prepare the withies in a small garden which he rented near the entrance to Coach Road. Opposite Prospect House is Harding's grocery and newsagent's shop.

71. *(Below)* My most vivid memory from early childhood is of stepping through the charred and stinking debris after Roy Harding's Bridge Street newsagents' shop was burnt down in 1956. I also remember hearing that Mr Harding had carried his two small sons to safety as the thatched building blazed around them. The building was replaced by Retsel House. Another Harding family shop, the Bristol Bazaar on the corner of Ricketts Lane and Market Cross, was burnt down in 1928.

72. J. Carpenter's (later F. G. and R. Rogers') baker's shop at Sturminster Market Cross in 1907. Posters in the window advertise Foster Clark's Jellies for a penny, two gallons of Eiffel Tower Lemonade for fourpence-halfpenny and the chance to make 15 buns for a penny using Eiffel Tower Bun Flour. The men are (from left) Randolph Rogers, Frank Rogers and Mr Carpenter.

73. Tom Rose and staff outside his butcher's shop on the south side of Sturminster Newton Market Place in about 1890. Mr Rose is the man in the centre; the others include Charlie Crew (left) and slaughterman Mr Nuth. The shop was originally the Market House and in the early 19th century housed two rows of stalls, mainly occupied by butchers. For most of the 20th century it has been a drapery store run successively by C. S. Hender, F. G. Moore and Alex J. Hicks. It is now Mounts' greengrocers' shop.

74. Stone and Rawles' Dorset Stores at Shillingstone in 1930. The shop is still a general store today.

75. Harding's horse-drawn delivery van at Hammoon in about 1900. "They brought groceries and paraffin from Sturminster Newton and kept the paraffin in a little cupboard on the back of the van," recalls villager Tom Hillier. "Another van came from Diffey's at Childe Okeford, driven by an old chap called Savoury." The woman in the doorway is thought to be Miss Maude Newman, who kept house for her father. The pair of thatched cottages in the background were burnt down about 1912.

76. The High Street, Okeford Fitzpaine, with Annie Trowbridge's general store on the left. Like many village shops, it stocked a remarkable range of products, including nails, pots and pans as well as groceries, sweets and tobacco. Annie even offered a boot repair service. She was known to villagers as Annie Plug; oddly, the premises are now an electrical shop!

77. The Cross, Okeford Fitzpaine, between the wars. The shop was kept by the Morley family. The telephone box was painted green instead of red at the insistence of local squire Mr Pitt-Rivers, whose influence also led to a grey call box at Hammoon. The colours were chosen to be more in keeping with the local environment.

78. Maidment's bakery van calls at one of East Stour's three village shops in 1910.

79. *(Above)* The Royal Mail van outside Marnhull Post Office in Burton Street about 1905. The van, drawn by two horses and driven by one Octavius Nicholas, travelled between Blandford and Henstridge via Marnhull each morning and evening. The postmaster was John White, who was also a draper and general shopkeeper. The goods advertised outside include Fry's Chocolate and Pure Cocoa, Anglo-Bavarian ales and stouts, Glen Castile whisky and Spey Royal. White's application for a licence to sell alcohol so offended the leader of Marnhull Congregational Church, John Galpin, that he refused to let the postmaster's daughter Clara White take her usual place at the church organ. When John White arrived, there was a violent struggle as he tried to remove Galpin from the organ stool by force, tearing his Sunday coat in the process.

80. *(Opposite page, top)* The Childe Okeford and Iwerne Minster Co-operative Stores in Upper Street, Childe Okeford, in the 1920s. Outwardly the premises have changed surprisingly little but they now offer teas and bed and breakfast.

81. *(Opposite page, bottom)* The village shop at King's Stag in 1906, when its stock included clothes, shoes, stationery, hardware, glass and china and groceries. The sign outside is an advertisement for Davis and Son, dyers and cleaners. It survived as a shop until November 1990. Next door (left) was Mogg's Bakery, recently opened as a general store following the closure of its neighbour.

82. Buckland Newton Post Office in 1910. The industrious postmaster George Mitchell was also a painter and clerk to the parish council.

83. Brewery wagons outside the Plough Inn at Manston at the beginning of the century. Both drivers are wearing leather aprons. The licensee was Arthur Courage. The Plough is thought to have been a farmhouse, then a cider house before becoming a fully-licensed pub. The dogs in the picture appear to be greyhounds, probably trained to hunt down rabbits and hares.

84. Stalbridge High Street in 1872 showing Wayside clothed in wooden scaffolding for major reconstruction work. By the turn of the century it was Mr Lake's barber's shop. The tall building on the right is Manchester House, part of Cox's drapery business where 14 girls lived in. Coxes also had soft furniture and tailoring shops opposite. In the distance is Grace's drapery, which provided fierce competition for the Cox business after young Mr Grace married one of the girls from Manchester House.

85. Stalbridge High Street in 1904. Miss Hatcher, the landlady's daughter, stands in the doorway of the Crown Inn. Opposite is Charles Meader's Old Curiosity Shop, a forerunner of the antique shops of today. The two ladies in black are thought to be the Curtis sisters. The man in the road is Mr Senior, who sold pig and poultry food from a shop on the right.

86. Bakery foreman Bill Orchard with Dikes' delivery cart at Stalbridge in 1912. Bill worked for Dikes for 30 years and had to keep an eye on the horse, Ginger Jack, who had a fondness for nibbling people's shoulders! Dike and Son was founded by Henry Dike and his wife in 1880 and before the First World War was one of four bakeries in Stalbridge. Today the business is run by their great-grandsons William and Frank Dike, who have 100 employees, 14 vans delivering over a 30-mile radius and shops at Stalbridge, Blandford and Castle Cary.

87. Butcher Frank Witt with the delivery cart from Short and Son's shop opposite the Market Cross at Sturminster Newton.

Travel and Transport

88. Off to Stur! Fiddleford farmer Harry Rose heads for the market town in his pony and trap in the 1920s. In the distance a car approaches. My late grandmother used to tell how Mr Rose once asked her to call Mumford the vet' at Sturminster on the newly-installed telephone at Fiddleford Post Office; then he rode to Sturminster in his pony and trap to check that the message had been received!

89. *(Left)* John Wilkins of Marnhull and his two-and-a-half horse power Sparkbrook motor cycle in about 1924.

90. *(Below)* W. Plowman and Sons' baker's van at Marnhull in 1922. Plowmans' shop in Pilwell closed in the mid-1950s. David Wilkins recalls that during the Second World War, when clothing was rationed, the owners raided their attic for garments from the Great War and sold them.

91. Mr Sharpe of Marnhull with his horse and trap in about 1900. He was connected with a slaughterhouse at Gannets, between Marnhull and Todber, and used to drive the trap as far as Wimborne to buy cattle for slaughter.

92. A covered carrier's cart makes its way past Marnhull Church and Rectory at the turn of the century. Its regular drivers were Levi Warren and Walter Drew, whose service connected Marnhull with Sturminster Newton railway station.

93. Charles Meader and family with their bicycles at Stalbridge in about 1900. By the turn of the century pedal power was a popular means of personal transport and penny-farthings and Victorian boneshakers had given way to cycles resembling the sophisticated machines of today.

94, 95. Horse power ancient and modern — two forms of personal transport on the roads of the Blackmore Vale. The horseman is Jack Frizell of Glanville's Wootton, who died within a few years of this picture being taken; the motorist, pictured at Stock Gaylard, is Howard Mogg, who ran the bakery at King's Stag. His car is a 25 horse power Scout, made near Salisbury by Albert Burden's Scout Motor Company. The firm was founded in 1902 to make motor-boat engines and within five years had a 70-strong workforce producing two cars a week. "How to Fly, purchase a Scout Car," read the early advertisements. "They simply fly up hills in top gear and skim along the ground like a bird." A switch to the production of mines during the First World War crippled the company's output and when the war was over it was unable to compete with the cheaper mass-production cars coming on to the market. Production ceased in 1922 and Scout cars are now extremely rare.

96. *(Above)* Three cars and a horse and wagon outside the Green Man at King's Stag in about 1908. Two of the cars are Fiats – the one on the left belonged to Sir Randolf Baker of the Ranston Estate at Shroton, the one on the right to Mr Francis Learworth of Hanford.

97. *(Left)* The streets of Marnhull get their first coating of tar and gravel in the 1930s. "The tar pot was drawn by a horse and the drums of tar were hoisted up and poured into a vat," recalls David Wilkins. "There was a fire below which made it thin and runny. A hosepipe sprayed it, gravel was thrown on it and then it was steamrollered. The work caused great excitement in the village."

98. *(Following page)* Road workers at Sturminster Newton with their steam roller and horse-drawn water cart. The rise of the motor vehicle produced a frenzy of road-surfacing between the two world wars.

99. The Knight family with their vehicles at the Excelsior Garage, Partway, Hazelbury Bryan, in 1945. The soldier and his army lorry are probably from the wartime searchlight base situated in a field behind the garage.

100. Pulham Garage in 1937 with mechanics Ron Barter (left) and Bob Hunt (centre) and owner John Spong. The car is Mr Wilcox's Morris 12 from Holwell. During World War II Mr Spong used to buy cars from London auction rooms for a fiver, fix pronged hay sweeps to them and resell them at a profit to tractor-starved Dorset farmers. "In some cases we used to take the bodies off and the farmers would sit up on the seat on the bare chassis," Ron Barter recalls.

101. Members of Hazelbury Bryan Methodist Church on their annual outing – probably to Weymouth or Bournemouth – in about 1920. At the wheel (far right) is Fred Knight, founder of Hazelbury's bus and coach company and one of the Blackmore Vale's first charabanc owners. The Model T Ford was known as "I Don't Know" on account of Knight's reply when friends asked him what he planned to call the brand new vehicle. Others in the picture include the Fifehead Neville miller Frank Clarke (standing, third from left) and Knight's father-in-law Tom Rolls (seated, second right).

102. Childe Okeford villagers set off on their annual outing in the charabanc Sturminster Queen in 1926, unaware that the first chapter of a remarkable romance is unfolding in their midst. Among them are young Henry Foot of Bishops Caundle (standing, far left) and May Wallbridge (seated), whose courtship ended after he proposed marriage and a new life in America and she turned him down. Henry went to Philadelphia, became a fireman and married an American girl; May also married but stayed in Dorset. In 1969, following his wife's death, Henry returned to England and was introduced to May who by then was also widowed. They married within a year and lived happily near Wimborne until Henry's death in 1990. May now lives at Verwood.

103. A goods train at Shillingstone station in 1904. Like the rest of the much-loved Somerset and Dorset, it was closed in 1966 by Dr Beeching, who is spoken of in these parts as they used to speak of Judge Jeffreys.

104. Stalbridge railway station and level crossing in about 1905. Industry has now taken over the site and railway remnants are difficult to spot.

Servicing the Vale

105. Piped water comes to Sturminster Newton in 1906. The water was held up at the mill to provide a dry river bed for the workmen.

106. Members of Marnhull Parish Council in 1940. They included a fireman, two policemen and a member of the Home Guard.

107. *(Left)* The village bobby on patrol in Lower Street, Okeford Fitzpaine, about 1920. The police house was subsequently built on the site to the right of the picture. The tumbledown shed in the background was the meeting place of the village slate club.

108. *(Below)* District Nurse Heffer with her caravan home, bell tent and Royal Enfield motor cycle in about 1930. She lived at Henley, Buckland Newton, and attended patients in several neighbouring villages. District nurses were employed by nursing associations to which their patients paid a fee or regular subscription.

109. Members of the Sturminster Urban District Fire Brigade proudly show off their first fire engine in the 1926 carnival procession. The 1923 Thornycroft engine is towing an old steamer pump bought from the Bryanston Estate in 1925. The crew includes Tom Crew (far left), Harry Peck, Mr Hallett and Bert Miles (front seat). The boy in the cap (foreground) is Jim Seal.

110. Sturminster Newton takes delivery of its brand new Austin ambulance in 1935.

The Vale at Play

111. Carnival queens of yesteryear join the procession for Sturminster Newton's 40th post-war carnival in 1990. Twenty-two of the 39 surviving queens took part in the procession, including the 1951 queen, Beryl Newman, who flew over from her home in the United States for the occasion.

112. A field opposite Sturminster Newton cemetery is the venue for this running race around a marked circuit in about 1910. Running races were popular as far back as the 18th century, when champions would be matched by their backers in the same way as horses.

113. There was a time when Grace and Hobbs opened the batting for Stalbridge. Not the legendary W. G. and Jack, of course, but Wilfred Grace and Leslie Hobbs, who played for the village side before the First World War. Leslie is in the centre of the back row in this picture, taken about 1910. The line-up where known is (back row, from left): Henry Hobbs, Galton the postmaster, Leslie Hobbs, –?, Mr Gant, umpire for 50 years; middle: Gary Meader, Eddie Dike, Goldsworthy the schoolmaster, –?, W. J. Dike; front: Harry Dike, –?, –?, F. C. Bollen the tailor, Habersham.

114. Soccer and cricket provided a sporting outlet for the rivalries which often existed between neighbouring towns and villages. This picture of Marnhull Football Club is thought to date from 1895.

115. Women's soccer was a rarity until recent years and this Marnhull ladies' team was probably formed for a special occasion such as the King's silver jubilee in 1935 or the coronation in 1937.

116. The Broad Oak Band, one of several bands in the Sturminster Newton area in Victorian and Edwardian times.

117. Summer garden parties have long been a feature of village life. This was one of many organised by the Rev and Mrs Samuel Hooper at Lydlinch Vicarage during the first quarter of the century. The Vicarage survives minus the tower, formerly used as servants' accommodation, and the verandah.

118. The circus comes to town – crossing Sturminster bridge in about 1930.

119. Boating on the Stour at Sturminster in 1907 – a popular pastime in Victorian and Edwardian times.

Special Days

120. Robert Young, friend of William Barnes and fellow dialect poet, at a flower show held in his honour as the oldest inhabitant of Sturminster Newton in 1907. He was 97. "He takes his daily walks and shows great interest in things in the town," says a contemporary report. "He forwarded £1 to Dr Barnardo's Home that day, the proceeds of his booklet." Young's humorous dialect verse appeared under the pseudonym Rabin Hill.

121. Marnhull's first old age pensioners outside the Post Office on January 1, 1909. To qualify for the first state pension of five shillings a week, they had to be over 70, have savings of less than £37 10s and have kept themselves out of the workhouse. Only two of the nine pensioners have been identified – Mrs Raikes (fifth from left) and Mrs Flooks (second right). The Postmaster (fourth right) was John White.

122. Members of Hazelbury Bryan Oddfellows and Slate Clubs pass through Wonston during their annual march with banners and band. Most towns and villages had a club or friendly society the main purpose of which was to provide support for members and their families if they were sick or died or in financial distress. Both the Hazelbury clubs had their headquarters at the Antelope.

123. The Marnhull Brass Band plays in the Rectory Gardens on Club Day before the Great War. Club Day was held on the last Wednesday in May and was a great occasion in Marnhull, with sideshows and merry-go-rounds and booths and stalls lining the road. Club members paraded through the village with flags, dancers and a band, calling at the Rectory and the two breweries. The original Marnhull Band dated back at least to 1850; there was also a Marnhull Fife and Drum Band for many years. The brass band – known as Star of the Vale – was formed in 1893 by Herbert Clark, who engaged a blind man from Sturminster, Johnny Wheeler, to instruct the players. Clark was succeeded by Harry Haskett, who was bandmaster until 1925 when the band broke up.

124. A band plays in the Square at Sturminster in 1910. Note that a single lamp has replaced the double one erected in 1902.

125. Members of the Ibberton Temperance Society prepare for their annual march through the village in about 1937. The temperance movement sprang up in the mid-19th century to counter the widespread problems of drunkenness and excessive spending on drink, which were seen as a primary cause of poverty and crime. Those pledging total abstinence publicly declared their stance by wearing a blue ribbon on their breast. Ibberton's society was launched in 1864. Later stalwarts included Edward King (pictured, centre, with walking stick) and John Sturmey (holding banner, left). The society was dissolved around 1950 and its funds and assets distributed among the church, chapel and village hall. Tradition has it that a final collection was also made around the village and the money used to finance an outing to Bristol Zoo.

126. A hero's welcome awaits someone at Hinton St Mary, though who and why we don't know. The date is 1906 or 1908. Even the pony pulling the trap is bedecked in flowers.

127. Maypole dancing at East Orchard about 1920. The origins of the May Day spring festival are lost in history and the Maypole itself has been with us at least 500 years. It was described in 1583 as "covered all over with flowers and herbs, bound round about with strings, from the top to the bottom, and some time painted with variable colours". The custom had declined by the 19th century, when William Barnes noted that Shillingstone "may now be the only Dorset village which keeps up the tall token of a merry May Day".

128. The Liberal MP for North Dorset, Mr A. W. Wills, pictured with his driver and supporters during the 1906 general election, when he polled 4,153 votes to his Tory opponent Sir Randolf Baker's 3,508. Wills was first elected at a by-election the previous year, when he defeated the same opponent by 909 votes.

129. The declaration of the poll in the Market Place at Sturminster in 1910. In the background is the former police station built on the site of Mitchell's soap and candle factory. In the mid-19th century Mr Mitchell used to give a special large candle to his customers at Christmas.

The Vale at War

130. The Blackmore Vale was not at war in 1910 but it must have seemed like it as thousands of troops occupied the outskirts of Sturminster Newton. The camp is in Durrant where around 200 tents were pitched during army manoeuvres.

132. *(Above)* The locals look on as troops of the Royal Horse Artillery clog Sturminster Market Cross during the 1910 manoeuvres.

131. *Opposite page)* Infantry on the march through Sturminster Square as war clouds gather in 1914. They may be the men of the Dorset Yeomanry, who set up camp in Durrant.

133. *(Following page)* Villagers gather outside the Crown at Marnhull for the departure of their husbands, sons and brothers following the outbreak of war in August 1914. For many the fond farewell was to prove all too final. Of the 190 Marnhull men who served in His Majesty's Forces during the First World War, 35 never returned. Others, doubtless, came home maimed or mentally scarred. Across the Vale and across the nation there was a similar story; in some places the statistics were signficantly worse.

134. Troops line the platform at Sturminster Newton railway station during the Great War. The railway was opened in 1863 and closed in 1966.

135. Cheesemakers at Hill View Dairies, Okeford Fitzpaine, in 1944, including four Italian prisoners-of-war brought from their camp at Motcombe each day to boost production. Many other captured Germans and Italians worked on the land. Also in the picture is my grandfather Jim Ridout (standing, third left), who was a cheesemaker at Okeford for most of his working life.

136. Like most towns and sizeable villages, Shillingstone had its own Home Guard unit during the Second World War. Originally called the Local Defence Volunteers, the Home Guard was organised in the spring of 1940 when there was every reason to expect a German invasion. Dorset initially had six battalions (later increased to seven), plus a Motor Transport Company. Despite the good-natured mockery associated with its Dad's Army image, life in the Home Guard was a serious business involving long and frequent training exercises for men who in most cases already had important full-time jobs.

137. *(Above)* Land Army girls Grace (top left) and Edith share harvesting duties with the locals in Mr Stride's field at Gains Cross, Shillingstone, in 1941 or 1942. The others include John Saunders (top centre), who was working out his war as a conscientious objector, and (bottom left) Arthur Field, well-known today as a leading figure of the steam fair fraternity. He identifies the machinery as a Marshall thresher and a Case LA tractor. Each sack contains a back-breaking two-and-a-quarter hundredweight, which was then the standard weight for wheat.

138. *(Opposite page)* The hounds of the Portman Hunt meet at the Plough Inn, Manston, in the 1920s. The kennel huntsman is Oliver Moss, who was the Portman's first whipper-in. He was killed in the Second World War.

Village Life

139. *(Left)* Children gather at Shillingstone village cross in about 1913. "The very beautiful and graceful village cross has been restored, indeed made new as a Jubilee Memorial," wrote Sir Frederick Treves a few years earlier. "It stands in the roadway, a delicate Gothic pinnacle, with an orchard and a thatched cottage for a background."

140. *(Below)* The main road through Shillingstone at the turn of the century with the New Ox Inn on the right. The thatched cottages next door were demolished between the two world wars.

141 Stalbridge High Street showing the present Crown Inn, which replaced an earlier thatched building. The event is the annual Club Day parade. Stalbridge Club Day was held each May and is described by Percy Dike as "a time for feasting with plenty of meats and cider".

142. A Model T Ford parked at Wonston, Hazelbury Bryan, in about 1920. The building jutting out on the right is now the village Post Office. The house on the left replaced the Old Bakery, which was burnt down. Ford's first "Tin Lizzie", as the Model T became known, was unveiled amid a blaze of publicity in 1908. Its success was immediate and phenomenal and 15 million cars eventually came off the production line.

143. A view looking down Crown Road, Marnhull, from the church tower. The thatched building on the left is the Crown Inn which Thomas Hardy called the Pure Drop in *Tess of the Durbervilles*. The picture dates from about 1907 when the Crown had a weighbridge in a little brick house at the side of the pub.

144. The Cross at Childe Okeford in about 1913. Tradition has it that the block of stone on the right was actually incorporated into the base of the memorial when it was built on the same site soon after the First World War. The Baker's Arms is on the right and next door is Dyer's the butchers, who had their own slaughterhouse behind the pub. Beyond Dyer's was Cottle's saddlery.

Okeford Fitzpaine.

G. Trowbridge
Okeford.

145. An agricultural roller outside the Royal Oak at Okeford Fitzpaine in 1915. The licensee was Elizabeth Steele who had succeeded her husband Edward. Their predecessor Thomas Dewfall quaintly advertised himself as a "fruit merchant amongst the Dorsetshire hills; every accommodation for visitors; good stabling; parties catered for at reasonable charges".

146. Collecting water from the River Divelish at the medieval packhorse bridge and ford at Fifehead Neville. The trickle of water is deceptive for the ford is an "Irish bridge", meaning that it has pipes beneath it to carry the water under the road in dry weather.

147. Bishop's Caundle gets a taste of things to come as a motor car joins two cyclists on the road through the village in about 1938.

148. Ambrose Stainer carries two pails of water through Stourton Caundle in 1929. "I can tell from the watering can in one of the buckets that he was fetching water from the brook to water the garden," says his daughter Enid Knott. "On washday you used to have to go half-a-mile to fetch water from a well." The scene has changed surprisingly little in 40 years – the bridge wall, farmhouse and tree (right), the Trooper Inn (left) and the house beyond the tree all survive.

149. Ibberton in about 1920 looking towards the foothills of Bulbarrow. The village remains a rural backwater but is not immune from 20th century change. The lime tree in the centre has gone; the village shop behind it has long since closed and the bakery in the shed next door closed in 1916. The thatched cottages on the right were demolished soon after the Second World War and replaced by a bungalow. The Wesleyan chapel in the distance has since been both a garage and a henhouse and is now a private dwelling called Wesley. Tradition has it that it was built by a local farmer who wanted an alternative place of worship after falling out with the village parson.

150. Bagber is famous as the birthplace of William Barnes the poet but even when this picture was taken about 1904 the farmhouse whose walls witnessed the event a century earlier had long since disappeared. The villagers and their cart horses are standing in what is now the busy A357 road. The house in the foreground is derelict and due for demolition; the house in the background – formerly Newmans Farm – survives.

151, 152. Two seasonal contrasts. A wintery scene at Hinton St Mary in *1909*, and haymaking near Sturminster Newton bridge in *1915*.